i'm broke!

the money ha

Liam Croke

ticktock

Copyright © ticktock Entertainment Ltd 2009

First published in Great Britain in 2009 by ticktock Media Ltd,
The Old Sawmill, 103 Goods Station Road, Tunbridge Wells, Kent, TN1 2DP

ticktock project editor: Victoria Garrard
ticktock project designer: Sara Greasley
With thanks to P J White and the Financial Services Authority

ISBN-13: 978-1-84696-952-2 pbk
Printed in China
9 8 7 6 5 4 3 2 1

Picture credits (t=top; b=bottom; c=centre; l=left; r=right):
Getty Images: 13c. Sebastiao Moreira/epa/Corbis: 38t. Shutterstock: 1, 2, 4, 5b, 6, 8,
9,10, 12, 13b, 14 both, 16, 18, 19, 20 both, 21, 23b 24, 25, 26, 27 both, 30t, 31, 33t, 34,
37, 38 both, 40, 41, 46, 47. Sipa Press/Rex Features: 13t. Hayley Terry & Sara
Greasley: OFCb, 7, 11, 21b, 23t, 30b 39 both, 43 both, OBCb both. ticktock Media
Archive: OFCt, OBCt. Worldwide Treasure Bureau: 5t.

Every effort has been made to trace copyright holders, and we apologise in advance
for any omissions. We would be pleased to insert the appropriate acknowledgments
in any subsequent edition of this publication.

contents

introduction

What is there to learn about money? I see something I want and I buy it. How simple is that?!

Well hold on there a second, money can get more difficult than that. It involves more than buying things. You have to think about needs and wants, saving and budgeting, taxes, different currencies and their value, consumers, producers, stocks, shares and so on.

In this book you're going to learn all about borrowing money, how to make money, and the many choices that are available to you when it comes to managing your money.

You may think you don't need to worry about any of this stuff yet, but you'll be surprised how valuable this new-found knowledge is going to be. The more you know about money, the more of it you'll have for the things you want – now and in the future.

Why and how was money invented?

- Thousands of years ago there were no shopping malls, no cars and no computers, so there was very little need for money.
- People traded and swapped with each other for things they needed or wanted such as clothes or food.
- It became apparent, however, that not everyone could trade or swap with each other as it was very difficult to agree on the value of items.
- An idea was put forward to use lumps of metal such as gold or silver as a common measure of value.
- Great idea but there was one problem: you had to weigh them to tell how much they were worth.

- How do you think this problem was overcome?

- Have a look at 2 different coins for a clue. What is different? What is stamped on them?

- Numbers of course!

- The number on each piece of metal shows what it is worth. The more precious the metal, the more value the coin has.

Did you know?

One of the first people to use coins as a means of currency were an ancient people called the Sumerians. They lived in a place called Mesopotamia nearly 5,000 years ago. The coins were cut from cone-shaped sea shells.

The Introduction of Paper Money

- In 1295 the explorer Marco Polo returned to Italy from an expedition to China with some amazing news: China had been using money, but it was in the form of paper!

- Because there were so many people living in China at the time and not enough metal to make coins for them all, people decided to make money out of paper.

- As with coins, they put a number on the paper to show how much it was worth.

tax

Can you imagine your life without money?

How do you think you would pay for food, clothes, magazines, DVDs, CDs? We take it for granted a bit don't we?

When you think about it you need money for just about everything – you need it to buy goods, you need it to pay for a place to live in, you need it for travel fares – in fact it is hard to think of anything that you don't need money for!

Where does all the money come from?

- Your local council pays for things such as new roads, the upkeep of your local park, playgrounds, decorations and lighting at Christmas time.
- The government of your country spends money on things for you, including teachers, schools, new hospitals and the police force.
- Where does all the money come from to pay for these things? Some comes from taxes. This is money governments collect from people and businesses. Governments also borrow money in order to pay for other things.

Did you know?

There is no age limit when it comes to paying tax. If you earn over a certain amount in a year, you must pay tax!

Did you know?

In the UK, 20p goes to the government in tax from every £1 you earn up to an income of £34,800. Above that amount 40p is taken from every £1 earned.

Who said that?

"The hardest thing in the world to understand is income tax."

Albert Einstein

National Insurance

- When you enter the workforce, either as an employee or if you start your own business, if you are over 16 years of age and earning a certain amount of income each week (over £105) then you have to make what are called National Insurance Contributions.

- You pay National Insurance Contributions (NICs) in order to qualify for benefits such as the state pension, certain illness or disability payments, payments to widows and widowers and so on.

- If you have two jobs with two different employers then each employer has to deduct NICs if the amount you earn with both or either of them is above a certain amount.

budgets and values

How does a government decide how much tax people and companies should pay?

They need to look at two things:

1) How much money they need
2) How much people can afford to give them.

It's as simple as that. The government will make a budget estimating how much money it will need to run the country for say the next three years. They then must decide how much of this money can be collected in taxes, and how much they should borrow.

Budget balancing

Setting taxes is quite a balancing act:

- If taxes are set too high then people will have less money to spend.

- If they are set too low then the government will not have enough money to spend on essentials such as schools, new roads and hospitals.

Different Countries, Different Currencies

When you go on your summer holidays, you may be going to a country that has a different currency to yours so you are going to have to change your money into that country's currency if you want to buy anything.

- When you go to the bank to get your dollars, euros, yen or whatever, the value of currency in each country might be different.

- For example, if you were changing one UK pound into Euros you might get two Euros in return.

Foreign Exchange

So, who sets the value of currencies?

- The value of one currency against another is called the exchange rate, and this rate is determined on what's called the foreign exchange market.

- This is the place where foreign exchange dealers in cities like New York, London, and Tokyo trade money in different currencies with each other.

Find the best deal

If you were to buy a new games console, where do you think you would get the best value for your money?

Suppose it costs:
- £130 Sterling
- €200 Euros
- $350 Dollars
- ¥34,000 Japanese Yen

Look in a recent newspaper or online to find the currency exchange rates for each of them. Where can you get the best deal?

9

the economy

Everyone talks about 'The Economy' but I don't really understand what it is!

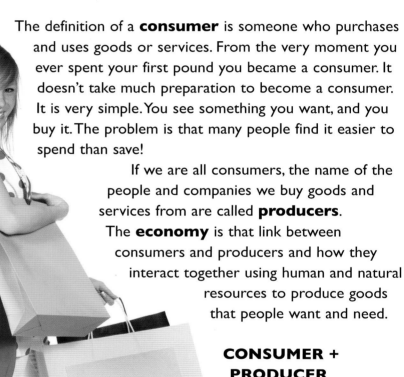

The definition of a **consumer** is someone who purchases and uses goods or services. From the very moment you ever spent your first pound you became a consumer. It doesn't take much preparation to become a consumer. It is very simple. You see something you want, and you buy it. The problem is that many people find it easier to spend than save!

If we are all consumers, the name of the people and companies we buy goods and services from are called **producers**. The **economy** is that link between consumers and producers and how they interact together using human and natural resources to produce goods that people want and need.

**CONSUMER +
PRODUCER
= ECONOMY**

Did you know?

A business is an enterprise that brings in money by selling goods or services.

Who said that?

"All achievements, all earned riches, have their beginning in an idea."

Napoleon Hill, best-selling self-improvement author of the early twentieth century.

Did you know?

The world's economies include the least populated country in the whole world – Tuvalu (a small island near Australia) with a population of less than 11,500 people – as well as China, the most populated country in the world with over 1.3 billion people.

I'm broke – how can I make my own money?

OK, so we know that you are a consumer, which is easy – all you have to do is buy goods or services. But what about becoming a producer?

Why not try...
Becoming a producer by starting your own business! By choosing something you love to do, it won't feel like work. How about...

- Getting crafty and making cards or knitting scarfs
- Baking cakes or cookies
- Selling on eBay™ (you will need your parents' help to set up an account if you're under 18).

entrepreneurs

Have you ever had an idea to start your own business?

If you have then you are not alone. An entrepreneur is someone who thinks up an idea that then becomes a business. They then hire workers to help with their idea.

Who said that?

"I never perfected an invention that I did not think about in terms of service it might give others… I find out what the world needs, then I proceed to invent it."

Thomas Edison, American inventor and businessman.

Risky Business

Entrepreneurs are often called risk-takers because starting a business is very hard work. It takes a lot of imagination, belief, talent, energy and courage to make a business successful.

Three top entrepreneurs

Walt Disney (1901–1966)

- Walt is the man behind one of the most recognisable brands and products in the world today.
- He started his own animation business at the age of 19.
- In 2007 the Walt Disney company made over £2 billion.

Roman Abramovich (born 1966)

- Orphaned at the age of 3, Roman grew up with his grandparents near the Arctic Circle.
- Using a wedding gift of around £1000 from his in-laws, he set up as a market-trader in 1987.
- His first business was selling plastic ducks from a Moscow apartment.
- Later businesses included pig farms, but the majority of his wealth came from a number of oil companies.
- In 2003 he became the owner of Chelsea Football Club and has since spent over £600 million on the club.
- He is estimated to be worth about £12 billion.

Sir Richard Branson (born 1950)

- His first two businesses failed (growing Xmas trees and raising budgies), but by the age of 20 he founded a small mail order retailer called Virgin.
- By 1984 he founded Virgin Atlantic Airlines and by 1997 he went into the train industry.
- His next idea is to take customers of his into suborbital space.
- He is estimated to be worth about £4 billion.

starting a business

How will you know if your new business will be successful? Remember, what you think is a good idea may not be to others!

Market Survey

One way of finding out if people will like your idea is to ask them!

- Carry out a market survey which asks people questions about what they like and don't like.
- A market survey asks people what products or services they would use and what they would be willing to pay for them.
- Reviewing the answers people give will help you decide whether you should proceed with your plans.

Window Cleaning Business

Let's assume you wanted to start a window cleaning service. You have the time, enjoy doing it and are good at it, but you're not 100% sure if the people where you live need or want these services. To find out, you could write a market research survey which might look like this:

Market Survey

	Yes	No
1) Do you wash your windows once a week?		
2) When you come home from work are you often too tired to wash them?		
3) Are those upstairs windows just too high up and difficult to clean?		
4) Would you like someone to wash your windows for you?		
5) Would you pay for this service?		
6) Do you know others who would also be interested in this service?		

Business plan

The results from your market survey were good so you decide to start your business. What's missing is your business plan.
This will tell you:

- what your service is
- who your customers will be
- how much it will cost to set up and run this business
- how much you can expect to make.

When you write a business plan

- Keep it concise and be realistic.
- Don't overstate anything – remember people reading your plan must see that you have done your research and analysis and that you understand your business.
- Remember to be aware of your competition and try and learn from them. See what they do best and understand why they do it well.
- Who are your main target customers, what are their needs, and how are you going to tell them about your product or service? (This is called marketing by the way.)
- When you work out the answers to these questions, you are well on your way to making sales.
- Remember, if you fail to plan, you plan to fail!

getting a job

If you're not quite ready to start your own business, there are many jobs you can find … or even start yourself.

Here are just a few which might appeal to you and get you thinking:

- Sports coaching
- Car washing
- Tutoring
- Lifeguard
- Washing neighbours' cars
- Dog walking or pet care
- House painting
- Tourist attraction jobs
- Grass cutting
- Babysitting
- Working in your favourite shop – you'll get some great staff discounts!
- Caddying at a golf course

Did you know?

You're not allowed to work after 7pm until you're 16 years old!

The rules

For your protection, there are regulations on the hours you are allowed to work:

- It is illegal to employ anyone under the age of 13 in the UK.
- There are very strict laws and guidelines regarding this and the Government is in no doubt what those over the age of 13 are allowed to do.

If you're 13 or 14:

- No more than two hours of work per day during term time.
- Five hours is allowed on Saturday.
- No more than two are allowed on a Sunday, and you are only allowed to work between 7am and 7pm, and between 7am and 11am on a Sunday.

If you're 15 or 16 (and of compulsory school age):

- Up to 12 hours work each week during term time.
- No more than 35 hours each week during the summer holiday.

Are there any places i'm not allowed to work?

If you're under the age of 18 you are not allowed to work in:

- commercial kitchens
- butchers or abattoirs
- rubbish collection
- amusement arcades

Although there is not a list of jobs teenagers are allowed to work at, it is widely accepted that shop work, hairdressing salons, office work, café and hotel work is permitted.

Remember!

No matter what job you get, it must meet safety regulations. All employers are responsible for ensuring your safety and working hours stay within legal requirements.

banks

My money's burning a hole in my pocket. What can I do to stop myself spending it?

So you are getting a weekly allowance from your parents, you are earning money from a part-time job, or maybe a combination of both. Now what are you going to do with it? Spend it all, or put some of it away where it is safe and earning money for you?

How about opening a bank account and putting it there? This is a great idea and a fantastic way to get serious about saving.

When did the banking system start?

Before you do anything let's first take a brief look at how banks first came into existence.

- Banks are as old as money itself, and records dating back nearly 2,000 years show the first deposits into banks.
- Temples and palaces were originally used as banks because they were well-built and busy places.
- Traditionally, the purpose of a bank was to loan money to companies – services for individuals came later.

Banks as businesses

- Besides keeping your money in a safe place, banks exist to make money.
- Banks are very much like any other business in that they want to make a profit.
- They do this by charging fees for the services they provide, and also they charge interest on loans taken out by customers.
- Banks aim to make a profit by attracting as many new customers as possible.
- How do they do this? Simply by providing services and accounts they think will attract new customers.

What services do banks provide?

- Savings accounts
- Current accounts (cheque books and debit cards)
- Mortgages (loans to purchase a property)
- Credit cards
- Car loans
- Foreign exchange
- Student loans
- Debit/Cash cards
- Commercial loans (loans for start up and existing businesses – this facility allows many companies to expand their business, which without a bank's money they would be unable to do)
- Online banking
- Bill payments – direct debits or standing orders which allow a certain amount of money to be deducted from your account at regular intervals to pay bills

- Stockbroking service – buying and selling shares

bank accounts

How do I open a bank account?

In order to open a bank account you will need to prove

(a) who you are and

(b) where you live.

It is likely that you will need a parent with you when opening an account, and they will need a copy of their passport or driver's license, a utility bill confirming your address and your birth certificate.

Once you have all of these documents, you are good to go. One last thing: don't forget to bring money with you!

How safe is my money?

The chance of a bank going bust is very, very slim. However, it is still important to know that if anything did go wrong you are still protected.

- The Financial Services Compensation Scheme insures individual accounts up to £50,000.
- This insurance applies only to banks and firms which are authorised by the Financial Services Authority.

Internet Banking

You are probably no stranger to surfing the net, emailing or blogging. But did you know that you can now do almost all of your banking from the comfort of your own PC?

Online banking has become very popular in recent years because:

- it's convenient
- it's quick
- it helps you to manage your money
- it ensures you pay your bills on time
- it is accessible 24 hours a day, seven days a week.

What do I need to do?

You can access your account information via your bank's website. Once you are set up and have your own personal logon password, you are good to go. Whenever you want to check your account balance or transfer money from one account to another, it's no problem – you can log on at any time of the day or night.

Did you know?

Transactions at cash machines cost a bank a lot less than doing business in a branch. This is why we're all using plastic more and can now do so much of our banking online.

Who said that?

"I rob banks because that's where the money is."

Willie Sutton, America's most daring bank robber.

interest

I've heard of people getting rich from interest alone. Is that possible?

- If you keep your money in a bank it will earn interest and will grow and grow because of a process called 'compounding'.
- When they add interest to your savings account, you begin to earn interest on the interest.
- Let's assume you have £1,000 earning 5% each year, then at the end of the year you would have earned £50 in interest.
- So, in year 2 you would have £1,050 in your account, again earning interest of 5% giving you £52.50 at the end of the year. Year 3 you would earn £55.13, Year 4 £57.88, and so on.

Look at it grow!

Year	Balance	Interest Rate of 5%
1	£1,000	£50
2	£1,050	£52.50
3	£1,102.50	£55.13
4	£1,157.63	£57.88
10	£1,551.33	£77.57
15	£1,979.93	£99.00
20	£2,526.95	£126.35

See how you begin in year 1 by just getting £50 added to your savings and end up with over £126 added? That is the magic of compounding and not only is your money growing, but the amount it is growing by is also growing!

Choosing the best account

- The competition between banks for your business is fierce.
- There are over 70 of them offering savings accounts.
- They want you to open an account with them so they can build a long term relationship with you. When you buy your first home, your first car or get your first credit card, they hope it is with them – the bank you opened your very first account with.
- So how do they do this? For starters, they offer very competitive rates of interest for your money on deposit. At the moment you can earn anything from 4% right up to 10%, so it is important to compare these rates, as well as the list of charges, before you decide which bank is best for you. Rates can quickly drop however so keep an eye on what rates your bank is offering to ensure they're competitive.
- Also, think about what you want from a bank, be it a branch local to you that is open on a Saturday or a phone or internet banking facility.

Did you know?

Most accounts come with incentives or offer free gifts. They range from vouchers, CDs, piggy banks, charts and stickers and many more. Try and look beyond these free gifts to make sure your money is working as hard as it can for you.

budgeting

I spend all my money straightaway and so am left with nothing. How can I make sure I save every month?

It is often said that "money makes the world go around" and you are certainly part of that world. Each and every day you spend your money on goods and services and as you get older and start to earn, more money passes through your hands so you need to learn to manage all your money.

Planning for the future

Look into that crystal ball of yours and think about where you want to be in five years time.

- Do you fancy travelling the world in your 'gap year'?
- Planning to go to college?
- Want to buy a car?
- Want to get your own place?

Whatever your goal is, you will need money to pay for it. So, if you want to achieve your goal you are going to have to plan and budget for it.

Learn to budget

A budget is a simple plan for saving and spending money. It can be money from your weekly allowance, money earned from your part-time job or other sources. Budgeting is a learning experience, but is a valuable and vital skill that will benefit you. It is something you will use for the rest of your life.

Where do I start?

- In essence a budget is looking at the money coming in and allocating that money out.
- You need to analyse exactly what your income and expenses are.
- Start by writing down all sources of your income each month on one side of a sheet of paper, and all your outgoings on the other side. It might look something like this:

Sources of Income	Per Month	Outgoings	Per Month
Allowance	£100	Cinema	£10
Part-time job	£100	CDs	£30
		Mobile phone	£40
		Food	£60
		Clothes	£40
		Magazines	£20
Total	£200	**Total**	£200

This is a great exercise as it will highlight to you exactly what you are spending your money on. You might always complain that you're 'broke' but is it any wonder if you are spending loads each month on your phone, fast-food or whatever?

Don't forget to save

- Of course, on the outgoings side there should also be money set aside for SAVINGS.
- If you don't set aside a little something each week or month, then that goal of yours is not going to happen.
- A budget is a great way of managing your money and avoiding debt in the future.
- Sure it takes a little bit of effort, but by doing it this way you won't come up short when you really need some cash.

spending

How can I become a smarter shopper?

Let me point out the obvious: making your money go a long way is a good thing. There is nothing uncool about looking for a good deal and saving a few pounds here and there. After all, this means that you will have more money left over for the things you need and want.

> ### Who said that?
>
> "A bargain is something you can't use at a price you can't resist."
>
> *Franklin Jones – author*

Smart spending

Making smarter spending decisions is just another way of finding more money without actually earning it.

Everyone loves to spend money and the reason given by most is because "it is fun". Spending money can be even better when it is carefully planned in advance, however. Why? It will help buy you even more.

Are you a smart spender?

You just got paid for babysitting your niece and it's time to spend your hard earned money. What do you do later that day?

A) Blow it all (and some more!) on that jacket you saw at the mall last weekend.

B) Check out the sales rack and buy a similar jacket to the expensive one but for a lot less money.

C) Window shop and decide to wait another week or so before making up your mind.

Are you a bargain hunter?

Which of the following sums you up?

A) I never wait for anything to go on sale. When I see something I like, I just have to have it.

B) I love 'buy one, get the second half price' but I always save 10% of my allowance each week.

C) I wait until an item is on sale and even then I try haggling with the sales assistant for a discount.

Turn the page to find out what sort of spender you are and how to fix any bad spending habits.

what sort of spender are you?

A answers

If you answered A to both of the questions you're a frivolous spender.

- You need to recognise your spending behaviour and start to make immediate changes if you want to avoid financial disaster now and in the future.
- You need to learn some self discipline. Try walking around a shop without buying anything. This will help curb those urges to buy things immediately.
- Open a bank account and start saving a little bit of your money each week.

B answers

If you answered B to both questions then you are smart spender and a bargain hunter – a top combination! You're very perceptive and it is time to teach others what you've learned!

C answers

If you have answered C to both questions then you're in danger of becoming a penny-pincher.

- It might be time to loosen the purse strings a little bit.
- It's important to enjoy your hard-earned cash and rather than hoarding all of it, enjoy spending some of it without feeling guilty.

How to Spend Less and Buy More – The 10 Golden Rules!

1) **Comparison shop before you spend.** Paying too much for something is the most common form of overspending.

2) **Be able to distinguish between 'needs' and 'wants'.**

3) **Learn how to make your money grow.** Set aside a certain percentage of your money each week into a savings account which will earn interest.

4) **Start budgeting today.** Write down exactly what you have saved, invested and spent each month.

5) **Look before you leap.** Don't get 'suckered' by adverts on TV or in newspapers. Learn to evaluate what is a bargain and what sounds too good to be true because you know what the answer is – it usually is too good to be true!

6) **Make a shopping list** before you go out and stick to it.

7) **When shopping only use cash.**

8) **Don't spend what you don't have.**

9) **Spend money thinking of your future** as well as your present.

10) **Always check if there's a student discount** and take advantage of them. Make the most of special offers and freebies.

Top Tip

Whether you are a good spender, a bad bargain hunter, or somewhere inbetween, one thing that should always remain constant is to keep a routine. Every time you get money, put some away.

pensions

Surely I'm too young to start thinking about a pension?

Not really. When you retire in about 50 years time you will need an income and a pension can provide you with that. Put simply, a pension is a long term savings plan that you cannot touch until you reach a certain age.

I know, I know, you have not even finished school yet and I am talking about you retiring, but bear with me. This is some of the most important financial advice you are ever going to get and I assure you, you will be glad when you are older that you listened to me.

But won't the government give me a pension?

- Yes, they will, but could you survive on £90.70 per week?
- This is the current state pension for a single person in the UK.
- What if you were used to earning £400 per week and then suddenly you're getting less than £100!
- What do you think would happen? No more foreign holidays? No more digital TV? No more shopping trips each weekend? No more meals in nice restaurants? Do you want to be watching your pounds and pennies every time you go out?

What do you do?

- Ideally you should start a pension when you start your first job.
- A little bit each month is fine. Start off slowly, but the important thing is to start.
- The longer you delay starting your pension, the more it will cost you.

Pension power

For example if you were earning £30,000 per year and you wanted a pension of half this amount when you retire, then the difference of how much you need to pay each month depending on age is huge!

Age	Cost per month
40	£470
20	£162

Top Tip

As you start to budget, plan to use 10% of your income for saving, 10% for investing, 10% for charity and the rest for spending.

credit cards

Credit means giving you money and allowing you time in which to repay it, usually with interest charged on the amount you borrow.

Pros and cons of credit cards

You're not allowed any sort of credit until you're 18, but it's important to realise that credit cards are neither good nor bad and have both pros and cons.

Pros

- They are a very convenient way to purchase items.
- They provide a way to manage your expenses each month.
- For things like booking a flight online, a hotel, a car and so on, they are almost impossible to do without.

Cons

- Credit card companies do not give you credit cards because of their good nature or generosity of spirit, they give them to you because they want you to use them so they can make money from you.
- If you don't repay the amount owed on time, all of the time, you will end up paying a lot of interest.

I've heard of people who got into debt because of credit cards, how does this happen?

- Once you get a card it is all too easy to use it and do so without keeping a track on your purchases.
- Credit card logos are in every shop we go into inviting us to spend whether we have cash in our wallets or not.
- Sometimes there is four weeks from the time we purchase to when we get our bill and in that time it's easy to pretend that the debt isn't real.
- When the bill does come in you have forgotten about those shoes, that sweater or that dinner out, and there is no way you can pay the bill in full, at least not this month.
- That is when the debt crisis begins to build.

What is the difference between a debit card and a credit card?

DEBIT means to 'subtract' so when you are using this type of card, you are subtracting money from your own bank account. It is still possible to become overdrawn when using a debit card however so be careful.

CREDIT is money that a bank is willing to give you, like a loan. What you must understand is that it is not your money you are spending. It belongs to the bank and you must know that you will have to repay the amount owed, plus interest if you do not pay in full each month!

Who said that?

"The only reason I made a commercial for American Express was to pay for my American Express bill."

Peter Ustinov, actor

Did you know?

If you had a credit card debt of £5,000, were 20 years of age and you paid the minimum amount each month, guess what age you would be when your debt was cleared in full? 46!!! In that time you would have paid over £7,000 in interest.

getting the best deal

The golden rule is to shop around!

Much like shopping for new clothes or a new bike, it is very wise to check with all the credit card providers to see what interest rate they are charging.

Money-making exercise

- Ask your parents what interest rate is being charged on their credit card.
- They're unlikely to know, so this is what you do: tell them that if you show them how to reduce their interest payments, can you, as a reward or commission—type payment, receive half of the difference they save?
- Tell them this is a 'win win' situation. Just look at how much you can save them if you can reduce their interest rate:

Decrease in interest by	£1,000 debt over 1 year	£5,000 debt over 3 years	£10,000 debt over 5 years
1%	Save £10	Save £151	Save £510
3%	Save £30	Save £463	Save £1,592
5%	Save £50	Save £788	Save £2,763
10%	Save £100	Save £1,655	Save £6,105
18%	Save £180	Save £3,215	Save £12,877

My Mum has a store card, is this the same as a credit card?

Store cards are a form of credit card. They are issued by, or for, a particular retailer and can only be used in that particular store.

Beware of store cards:

- If you use your store card to purchase goods you will be 'rewarded' with discounts or exclusive offers which is, of course, just another way of making you come back and spend more. You may end up spending more on things you don't really need or want just to build up rewards.

- Do not let a promise of a 10% discount lull you into agreeing to a lousy credit card deal. There is nothing rewarding about having your money sucked away by high interest rates.

- The interest rate on many store cards can be as much as 30%, twice the rate of a normal credit card!

Top Tip

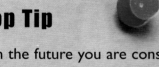

If in the future you are considering getting a store card, then only get one if you can pay your balance off in one go each and every month. That way you get all of the perks and don't have to pay interest.

Pre-paid Cards

You are not allowed a credit card of your own until you are over 18 years old, but did you know you can get a pre-paid card? It can be used in the same way as an ordinary credit card.

How does a pre-paid card work?

Very simply!

- You buy a card that has a predetermined amount of credit and you can use it until your credit runs out.

- It is very similar to a mobile phone card credit and is safer than carrying cash.

- The big advantage is that you can't overspend and rack up huge debts!

saving, investing and speculating

What's the difference between saving and investing?

Most people think that saving, investing and speculating is the same thing. This could not be further from the truth as they are very different and here is why:

Saving is when you put money, either by way of a lump sum or a set amount each month, into a risk-free financial product. It grows safely and slowly over time. An example of this would be a savings account in a bank.

Investing is when you put money into financial products where some degree of risk exists, but you are hoping that your money will grow significantly over time. An example of this would be buying stocks and shares.

Speculating is putting money into a financial product with a high degree of risk, hoping that your money will grow rapidly. You could put money in a new startup company that is developing experimental products or new technologies.

When you decide what you are going to do with your money, saving and investing will almost certainly be options to follow. Speculating might be a limited option.

What are shares?

- If you own shares, it means you own a share of a company so you become a shareholder.
- You are a part-owner of the company and you can have a say in how the company is run.
- Most companies will have an annual shareholders meeting, which you will be invited to. At this meeting the company's performance for the previous year will be discussed and plans for the future outlined.
- People buy stock with one goal in mind: to MAKE MONEY!

1) Buy Low
2) Sell High

Stock can go up as well as down!

Here is how it works. If you buy a particular stock at £1 and the company performs well, then you can expect the value of its shares to go up. So, if the price of that share you bought becomes £2 and you decide to sell it, then you have made a profit of £1.

Of course the reverse can also happen. If the price of a share goes down, then the value of your share also goes down. The secret is to buy a stock at a low price and sell when it's high.

Word of warning

If you don't know anything about the company you are going to invest in, then don't take a gamble on its shares unless you can afford to lose the money that you invest.

Reduce the risk and research!

It is a risky business buying and selling shares, but one way of reducing this risk is to do some research. Look at how the company has performed in the past, how long it has been around and how it compares to other companies.

what is the stock market?

Prices of stocks are determined by the stock market where they are bought and sold.

The value of stock may change on a daily basis. If a lot of people want to buy a particular stock the price will go up and if they want to sell, it will go down.

The UK has the FTSE100 and in the US there are several different stock markets such as the NASDAQ, the AMEX and the NYSE.

Did you know?

- A bull market is a period when the stock market does well and prices go up.

- A bear market is when the stock market is doing poorly and prices go down.

How do I buy and sell stocks?

You do this by using a stockbroker who buys and sells shares of stock for people. In return for this service, you pay a fee to them called commission.

Who said that?

"October: this is one of the particularly dangerous months to invest in stocks. Other dangerous months are July, January, September, April, November, May, March, June, December, August and February."

Mark Twain, author and humorist.

How long will it take me to become a millionaire?

- Maybe not as long as you think and with not as much money as you would think either!

- If you saved no more than £500 each year, starting at the age of 18, and earned 16% or more each year – which is quite possible with smart investing in stocks and shares – then you would become a millionaire in your 60s.

- So, by being smart, saving regularly and picking the right stocks, you can turn a few hundred pounds each year into a million in just a few decades.

- By the way, if you were to put this money into a bank and earn, lets say 4% each year, then you would become a millionaire as well. The only problem is you would be 130 years old by the time you hit the million mark!

loans

I've been told I should never take out a loan, are they really that bad?

At some stage in your life you are probably going to have to take out a loan for one reason or another. You may want to buy a car or a house, for example.

Did you know?

If you buy a TV for £2,000 and you borrow money at a rate of 15% over 5 years, do you know how much the TV ends up costing you? It will cost £2,855! So, why don't you just save the money each month instead until you have enough to buy it with cash?

Good Loans vs. Bad Loans

Some loans are better than others and I was once told you should only "borrow money to make money" and this is very true. A loan to buy a house could be classed as a 'good' loan because you are buying something that might go up in value. However if you borrow money to buy a plasma TV that would be considered a 'bad' loan because the TV has no resale value, and it is costing you a lot in terms of interest payments.

If I decide to go to university, how am I going to pay for it?

A student loan is also referred to as an educational loan. Furthering your education and obtaining a qualification is an investment in your future, so a loan to pay for university can be classed as a 'good' loan.

Student loans

Deciding to take on a student loan is probably the first major financial decision you are going to make. It requires research and an understanding of how you will pay it back.

- In the UK, financial support is available for full-time students to help with tuition fees, grants for living expenses and scholarships to universities and colleges.

- While grants don't have to be paid back, bear in mind that a student loan does. This is normally done after you have left college and are earning over a certain amount each year. At the moment this figure is £15,000.

- A scholarship on the other hand does not have to be repaid as they are given as grants to students who satisfy a number of requirements.

Five steps to a student loan

Arranging a student loan can be a complicated matter so it is important to get advice and do your research. Here are five things you should do before you take out a student loan:

- Start early – find out what grants you are entitled to at an early stage

- Search for 'free money' – apply for financial aids and scholarships

- Set up your budget

- Estimate just how much money you will need

- Decide on a loan from the government or a private loan arranged by your parents.

your credit rating

How you repay your loan has an impact on what is called your credit rating.

Be aware!

- When a bank decides to lend you money they do a 'credit check' on you which allows them to look at any loans you currently have or have had in the past.

- The credit report shows whether you repaid these loans on time as you promised when you originally took out the loan.

- If you are two or three months behind with repayments, or you fail to repay the loan at all, then this will have a serious impact on whether you get any loans in the future and what interest rate you will be offered.

- If you have a history of late payments then you are considered a 'high risk'.

- If you're 'high risk' a bank may still be willing to lend you money, but at a much higher rate than someone who repaid their loans on time.

The difference between a good credit rating and a bad one: A TRUE LIFE STORY

Let me give you an example of two friends I know who are currently purchasing exactly the same type of property, at exactly the same price and are borrowing exactly the same amount.

The first borrower, Fred, has an excellent repayment history and therefore has secured a mortgage with one bank without any difficulty and is being charged a rate of 5.15%.

The second borrower, Frank, took out a personal loan three years ago and missed a number of repayments for one reason or the other. His only option is to arrange his mortgage through what's called a sub–prime lender who is charging him a rate of 8.35%.

Guess what the difference is in monthly repayments between the two? Frank is paying **£655 more each month** because of his bad credit rating.

That is nearly an **extra £8,000 per year** all because he missed repayments on a personal loan he took out a few years back.

Now, had he known this was going to happen, I am sure he would not have missed a repayment here or there.

The moral of this story?

Don't ever become the person who pays £655 more each month. If you ever get a loan from a bank, repay it on time.

glossary

Annual Percentage Rate (APR) The percentage cost of credit charged on a yearly basis. For example, if you borrow £100 for a year at 10% APR then it will cost you £10 at the end of the year. Every loan has a specific APR so it is key to know the APR when comparing loans offered by different banks.

ATM card A debit/cash card that allows customers to withdraw money from an automated cash machine.

bank statement A summary of what went into and out of your account in a month.

bear market When the stock market is doing badly and prices are going down.

budget Plan for saving and spending money.

bull market When the stock market is doing well and prices are going up.

commission Fee paid for a financial service, eg buying and selling shares.

compound When interest you earn from a bank is added to your savings so your interest also begins to earn interest.

competition When other businesses are selling a product or service similar to yours.

consumer A person who buys and sells goods and services.

credit Money given that must be repaid, usually with interest.

credit card A card that allows you to buy things without having to use cash.

credit limit The maximum amount of money you are allowed to spend on a credit card.

debit card A card that allows you to withdraw money directly from your bank account.

debt Money owed to a person or business.

default The failure to repay a loan.

depression A period marked by high unemployment. Prices drop for goods, with no one willing to buy anything with what little money they have.

economy When human and natural resources interact to produce goods and services.

entrepreneur Someone who takes a risk in creating a new business, and introduces a product they believe will be innovative and something consumers will want to buy and use.

foreign exchange market Place where foreign exchange dealers in cities around the world trade with each other in different currencies.

income tax Tax deducted by the government on money earned from working.

inflation When things you buy cost more than they used to. They have increased or inflated in price.

interest Money a person has to pay when he/she borrows money or the money a bank pays to you when you have your money deposited with them.

market survey A series of questions asking people what they like and don't like, what services they would use, and what they would be willing to pay for it.

mortgage A loan given by a bank to pay for a house.

pension A savings plan for when you retire.

producer A person or business that provides goods and services.

profit The money a business makes after deducting the costs for making and selling the goods.

Personal Identification Number (PIN) The 'secret' number which allows you, and only you, to use your debit or credit card.

recession When fewer goods are being sold, leading to fewer goods being made, which leads to fewer workers being needed to make them, leading to large scale unemployment.

retirement When a person reaches a certain age and gives up their job.

savings Money put into a bank that can be used later for a holiday, college fees, or a deposit for a house. It is also used for a 'rainy day' i.e. periods of unemployment or when your income reduces.

shareholder Someone who owns stock in a company.

stock When you buy part of a company as an investment.

stockbroker A person who buys and sells shares for other people.

stock market A place where shares of stock from different companies can be bought and sold.

tax Money that people and businesses must pay to help support a Government.

further information

Childline
www.childline.org.uk
Advice website and helpline for anyone who is feeling scared or worried about something and needs to talk to someone in confidence.

Connexions
www.connexions-direct.com
Provides advice on money management and student finances.

Citizens Advice Bureau
www.citizensadvice.org.uk
The biggest provider of free advice on debt and money matters in the UK.

Office of Fair Trading
www.tradingstandards.gov.uk
Advice for consumers on buying and paying for products, including a helpline.

HM Revenue & Customs
www.hmrc.gov.uk/index.htm
Ensures the correct tax is paid by individuals and companies at the right time. It has a very good interactive resource on tax and public spending.

FSA

www.whataboutmoney.info/

The FSA is an independent body that regulates the financial services industry in the UK. They now have a site that offers advice specifically for young people.

Youth information

www.youthinformation.com

A fantastic and informative website that provides guidance and direction from employment and training, family and relationships to money, sport and leisure – check it out.